Contents

Prologue

Chapter 10: Therapy

Chapter 9: Mentorship/Guidance/Role Models

Chapter 8: Proper Perspective

Chapter 7: Educational Attainment

Chapter 6: Positive Reinforcement

Chapter 5: Faith & Character Builder

Chapter 4: Financial Attainment & Financial literacy

Chapter 3: Examples of others in similar pain/Interviews/stories

Chapter 2: Self-esteem/ Self-confidence

Chapter 1: Becoming the Parent/Leader you Wanted/Advice from me

Chapter 0: Sports Heaven versus Reality

Epic Dialogue: Epilogue

Prologue

"I became a man early"

That quote pretty much sums up how I have felt my entire life. My father died when I was 6 years old and my whole perspective on life changed. As a kid your life should be about unadulterated fun, not wondering what death is. I didn't even realize death was permanent until I was about 10 years old, so for many years I thought my dad was coming back.

Angry, sad, whatever negative emotion you can imagine I was experiencing them for years. I had a great mom, siblings, stepfather, grandparents, uncles, aunts, cousins, and friends who helped me during those trying times. However, sports became my main therapeutic remedy for the pain I was going through.

DISCLAIMER: The love I have for sports (mainly basketball, football, and baseball) may not apply to you; keep this in mind when reviewing this book. I am only responsible for telling you my accounts and views. Don't you wish everything had a DISCLAIMER you could notice?

You could change the title of this book to Education Heaven, Dance Heaven, Music Heaven, or any social entity preferable. But as long as you keep the Fatherless or motherless Child in the equation you will get the same answer: Someone who has found or is searching for a place of refuge from the pain of not having one (or both) of their parents.

I want to elaborate on the Fatherless/Motherless Child title also. Fatherless/Motherless Child does not just single out kids who have lost a parent(s) through death, abandonment, imprisonment, or neglect. There are some parents who are present physically in their children's lives but not emotionally and socially as their kids need them to be.

I know whenever I thought about a kid(s) with both parents who seemed to be doing well financially that those kids had everything life could offer. But I've witnessed many occasions where those kids were missing just as much from their living parents than I was missing from my deceased father.

Recently I was talking to my cousin Cledwin Berry when he asked what the book's main focus was and after I told him about the Fatherless/Motherless dynamic he then said to me: "Ant, I felt and still feel that same way about sports and you know I had two loving supportive parents." I understand there are a lot of people like Cledwin who love sports and have two great parents.

Believe me I thought about naming the book Sports Heaven: Why sports is like therapy and some other titles that included everybody who loves sports. But I wanted to write this book from the perspective of someone who has lost a parent or loved one from the reasons I mentioned before and has used sports to help them cope with the realities of life. There are millions of people who can relate and I wanted to write why I believe sports is an outlet for US.

There is also the fact that sports has taught me so many lessons and made me better at other aspects of my life. I'm not sure if I would have had the motivation to improve on certain things if I hadn't been involved with sports.

I know there are critics who say our society places too much emphasis on sports (especially in the inner city and low income areas) and I agree on certain points. I agree that if you have playing professional sports as your future career you better have a "plan b" because the odds are enormous. I agree that professional athletes should not be paid more than teachers, doctors, firefighters, and other important professions in our society. Which basically means those professions are underpaid, not that athletes are overpaid.

I also know that there are people who have had (or have) two loving supportive parents and sports is important in their lives as well. Sports also gives them the same benefits as it has given the fatherless/motherless children. But the purpose of this book is to explain WHY sports is important for kids who have experienced what I and so many others have experienced. WHY sports can be used in the healing process when dealing with so much pain and help someone move forward with their life to become the best person they can be…

SPORTS HEAVEN

Chapter 10: Therapy

"I had a good doctor: Dr. James Naismith! He invented basketball and basketball gave me therapy sessions"

Sports became my therapy in 1979, it was the year that: (1)Michigan State with Magic Johnson beat Indiana State with Larry Bird in the NCAA Championship game (2)Supersonics beat the Bullets in the NBA Championship (3)Steelers beat the Cowboys in the Super Bowl (4) Pirates beat the Orioles in the World Series.

I watched all of those events because my uncles James, George, and Tim Honablew were big sports fans and we watched the games at my grandparent's house. I learned a great deal about sports from my uncles and they taught me

SPORTS HEAVEN

about the value of hard work. There was always exciting dialogue (with a lot of curse words I must add) about what was going on in those games and it piqued my curiosity about sports.

After those events every chance I got I was playing basketball, football, and baseball or watching those sports on TV. I enjoyed playing them all but I fell in love with basketball and love was definitely what it was. It was the best feeling I had experienced up to that point. Whenever I felt sad, mad, or had any other problems I could go play or practice basketball and I would feel better.

When my father died on February 16, 1976 it felt like time stood still and I can vividly remember when my cousin Greta was trying to explain to me that he had died. I couldn't grasp what she was telling me and as I mentioned in the

SPORTS HEAVEN

beginning of the book I didn't know that death was permanent. Once I realized it was permanent the thought of not seeing him again hit me like a ton of bricks and it was definitely the worst feeling that I had up to that point in my life.

I'm sure most counselors would explain that after my father died getting "professional help" would have been the best method for me to deal with my feelings but I don't believe there would have been any therapy better than basketball. Better yet I didn't have to draw pictures or talk about my feelings, I could just enjoy the thrill of shooting the ball through the hoop or work on my dribbling skills.

Furthermore I don't recall anyone ever asking me about how I was dealing with my dad's death so basketball was my communication outlet. Maybe my family and friends thought they were doing me a favor by not asking me how I was feeling about my dad's death. But I needed something or someone to say "Life can bring about some terrible tragedies but everything is going to be okay."

Whenever I see someone who has experienced what I went through or a kid who is dealing with it I understand their emotions and feelings. Getting mad "at the drop of a hat", disregarding authority (especially certain males), combative, being distant, unmotivated, and many other negative actions I went through them all. But wasn't I supposed to? When you lose something as important as your father or mother "all hell breaks loose" and you better find a positive outlet or your life will be hell as well.

There are adults who lose a parent or parents and can't cope with that reality. So how is a kid going to deal with

SPORTS HEAVEN

that void? My belief is that if you can't get counseling from a "professional" then get therapy from something that removes all of the negative thoughts and replaces it with positive feelings. See what I did there? Positive feelings will overcome negative thoughts every time. Whatever your passion is then emerge yourself into it and allow your mind to receive some peace.

Playing sports or watching it made me forget about some of the things I was feeling bad about. Some people wonder why in the black community sports seems so important and one of the reasons is because a lot of kids are missing their fathers or both parents. Many of these athletes have also experienced the loss of close friends, family members, or loved ones without getting counseling for it.

If you go through NBA and NFL rosters you will not find

SPORTS HEAVEN

too many players who grew up with both parents. I'm willing to bet that most of them saw sports as therapy or their safe haven from their surroundings. I may be a little too optimistic but it is my hope that MOST of those players will become advocates in their communities and provide HOPE to kids who are experiencing the same things they did. They don't have to sell them the dream of being a professional athlete, sell them the reality of making your goals come true no matter the odds.

That's why I started the SportsDad Program so that those kids regardless of race or gender will know that there are adults who understand their pain and want to help them navigate through it because they've been through it. Losing a parent(s) or having a parent(s) not involved in your life causes a lifelong scar and it is something you never "get over."

SPORTS HEAVEN

I am 45 years of age right now and my father passed away 39 years ago but I still think about him every day. The toughest moments are when something good happens like the birth of children, graduations, or athletic achievements because those are the times when I wish my dad was here to witness those things in person.

I remember once telling Coach H.K. Harrison (Clinton Junior College) who was recruiting me at the time that "Basketball is my life" and it sounded good to him until he realized that I meant it. My senior year in high school he called me on the night of my then girlfriend's prom and asked me "Are you ready for the big night?" and I said "yeah I'm watching the Lakers playing the Mavericks right now in the Western Conference Finals." I didn't even go to the prom because I wanted to watch basketball and for the fact that I

SPORTS HEAVEN

didn't like the idea of spending the money for it.

Coach Harrison told me "Son I know you love basketball and I'm glad about that but you have to add some more things to your life or you'll be a lonely man all of your life." Needless to say I didn't keep that girlfriend that long after that happened but it didn't matter to me because I was on a mission to get a basketball scholarship.

I was fanatical when it came to basketball and there's no other way to describe it. I was a teenage boy with hormones raging but if you gave me a choice of chasing some pretty young girls or going to the gym to shoot hoops it would have been the gym every time. I am sure all of my friends and people who knew me would agree that is exactly how I was but they didn't understand why. It was therapy for me, basketball was my therapy for all of the pain I was going

SPORTS HEAVEN

through. I can't go out and play now like I used to but being around the game gives me the same positive feelings, especially teaching it.

An ironic thing with my father's death and how much basketball has played a major part in my life is that the man who accidentally killed my father used to attend all of my older brother Durrell's and my high school basketball games. I didn't even know how my dad died until I was 26 years old and an older friend of mine told me about it.

My friend was also the one who explained to me about the man attending our basketball games because doing that gave the guy some comfort in seeing us grow up and excel in sports.

Imagine the pain that man was going through and I had no idea. The basketball games must have been like therapy for

SPORTS HEAVEN

him too. I have never even spoken to the man about the incident because I didn't know but I felt so bad for him once I did find out. Not an ounce of animosity towards him at all and I pray that he has found something to help him deal with the tragedy as I have.

It may sound crazy to some people that basketball has played a huge part in me overcoming the loss of my father at such a young age but it's 100 percent true. It was important for my mental health which is something a lot of us take for granted. As a kid I didn't know what the term depression meant but I have seen it many times and I knew I didn't want that to overtake my life. A friend once asked me "how did you deal with your father's death at such a young age?" My answer "I had a good Doctor: Dr. James Naismith, he invented basketball and basketball gave me therapy sessions."

SPORTS HEAVEN

My dad William Edward Mercer before he died in 1976. For 44 years all I have remembered is the love he gave me.

SPORTS HEAVEN

Me at 5 years old, a couple of months before my dad died. The pic always reminds me of my innocence.

SPORTS HEAVEN

Chapter 9: Mentorship/Guidance/Role Models

"I look back at all the mentors/role models I had and they played a part in the positive way I look at life"

I was blessed to have a lot of positive role models around me growing up but some kids aren't that lucky. If you grow up in an environment where a lot of things you see are mostly negative, if you grow up without one parent present or any parents at all, if you grow up without any positive influences in your family…..then someone like that should look for good role models wherever they can find them.

Sometimes your role models are not in your house or your community and that is just a fact of life. My love of sports has allowed me to emulate positive things from various

SPORTS HEAVEN

professional athletes when I didn't see those things first hand. I was blessed to have some positive men in my life after the loss of my father but there were some things they didn't do like some of those professional athletes did.

Julius "Dr. J" Erving was the epitome of style and grace. Seeing him in commercials, movies, and the way he carried himself made me want to be like him. I also remember reading about his business deals with various companies and I thought "So you can play sports and be involved in business?"

Jim Brown may be known mostly for his great skills on the football fields but I also read about how he and Bill Russell (among many other professional athletes) were right by Muhammad Ali's side when he was protesting his entrance into the Army. Mr. Brown has also gone on to do many wonderful things in the community for African-American men.

SPORTS HEAVEN

Watching Coaches John Thompson and Lenny Wilkins put the idea in my mind that I could be a basketball coach one day. Coach Thompson also spoke his mind about things that he thought was unfair and I remember watching him when they showed him walking off the floor before games in protest.

Dean Smith, Nolan Richardson, Jerry Tarkanian("Tark" was one of my nicknames by the way), "Magic" Johnson, Nate "Tiny" Archibald(who actually came to one of my bball events to speak), Michael Jordan, Kareem Abdul-Jabbar, Clyde "Walt" Frazier, Lynn Swann, Ozzie Smith, were just a few of professional athletes or coaches that I perceived as role models.

Notice that all of the athletes I mentioned were positive guys, not perfect but they were positive in the ways they conducted themselves. I didn't have to know them personally but they made an impact with me in how they carried themselves and what other people said about them.

As I mentioned earlier I had the great pleasure of meeting Nate "Tiny" Archibald when he VOLUNTEERED to come and speak at an Exposure Basketball Event that I was conducting at Tarboro High School in Tarboro, North Carolina in September 2001.

Imagine that?! The guy I used to hear about as a kid and watched on TV. Who I patterned my game after because he was the only (and still to this day) NBA player to lead the league in scoring and assists in the same season, came and spoke at my event. I was in Sports Heaven that day for sure!

And it's not just professional athletes and coaches who can provide a positive role model for kids looking for one. I

SPORTS HEAVEN

have worked as a Physical Education teacher with kids from Pre-School to high school and I knew which kids were looking at me as someone positive. Especially those kids who were enduring what I went through, their actions showed it all.

I learned a great deal of how to conduct myself from watching a lot of positive coaches and athletes. One of the most important things I learned is that it's okay to speak your mind and be prepared for backlash. A lot of the positive traits I have come from watching those positive athletes who came before me.

When I first fell in love with basketball I also had my older brother Durrell and some other peers that I looked up to as mentors. Durrell was a very good high school basketball player and watching him made me want to do all of those things he was doing. The dunking part is something I really

SPORTS HEAVEN

wanted to do because my brother was dunking his junior year in high school and he was only 5'10.

He made the Tobacco Belt All-Conference team as a junior along with some of the best players in the state of North Carolina (Harry Burrus of Mattamuskeet and Brian Rowsom of Columbia were two of them). Durrell was also a standout football player (his senior year only) on Creswell High School's only team to make it to the state championship game. So I looked up to him a lot and it pushed me a great deal following in his footsteps as a basketball player.

My friend Brian Rowsom was the first player who made me believe that I could get a basketball scholarship. He was five years older than me but his grandparents lived right across the street from my grandmother in Columbia, North Carolina so that's how we became friends. He was like another

SPORTS HEAVEN

big brother to me and Brian was big in the literal sense. He was 6'8 in high school and was one of the best basketball players coming out of our area.

He went to UNC-Wilmington on a basketball scholarship where he grew to the height of 6'10 and became a College All-American his senior year. He was drafted by the Indiana Pacers in the 1987 NBA draft along with NBA legend Reggie Miller. Brian was also a member of the original Charlotte Hornets team. He was definitely a big inspiration for sure with basketball but he also conducted himself positively off the court, something I paid attention to.

Another peer who was instrumental in my growth with basketball and life was my friend Tony Midgett. Tony was a year older than me and also lived in Columbia near Brian. I went to school in Creswell, North Carolina which was

SPORTS HEAVEN

Columbia's rival. Creswell versus Columbia was like the Duke versus North Carolina rival on the high school level. My dad was from Columbia so I had a lot of family there and I spent a great deal of time there.

One of the issues I had growing up was having family and friends in Columbia that people in Creswell didn't get along with or vice versa. I spent many of my summers in Columbia learning how to play basketball from Tony and some of my other friends there. I watched EVERYTHING Tony did and it made me a better basketball player.

Tony was so relaxed on and off the court that there should be a documentary about him on how to maintain your composure in all situations. He used to chew bubble gum during games and I remember there was a picture where the camera man caught him blowing a bubble while he was

SPORTS HEAVEN

making a play on the court. The newspaper article stated "Michael Jordan & his tongue, Tony Midgett & his gum", the dude was super cool. When Tony received a scholarship to play basketball at Akron University with Coach Bob Huggins it was another revelation that I could do it too.

Two of my best friends had gotten basketball scholarships and they were guys who ALWAYS shared their knowledge with me about EVERYTHING. Their effect was more than basketball too, they were guys who didn't drink or smoke which is something I respected. It's always a good thing to have friends and mentors who will push you to be better or are good examples of what you want to be.

Even at a young age I saw some players who messed their lives up by drinking too much or getting addicted to drugs so I vowed that wouldn't happen to me. Len Bias was

SPORTS HEAVEN

one of my favorite players and after his tragic death, I promised myself and my grandmother Beulah (my dad's mom) that I would NEVER do drugs or become an alcoholic (promise kept).

I learned WHAT NOT TO DO from some players I grew up watching and that was an important part of the equation when making decisions outside of basketball. Michael "Sugar Ray" Richardson and Roy Tarpley are two names that come to my mind when I think about telling myself I wouldn't get involved with drugs or alcohol. They were great basketball players but those things curtailed their careers and I didn't want something like that to take over my life.

There were also people who weren't family or friends but they gave me encouraging words when they saw me because they wanted me to "make something" out of my life

SPORTS HEAVEN

or go somewhere where there were more opportunities to succeed. There were numerous people who acted as protectors to keep negative influences from creeping into my life or prevented something that could have derailed my future.

I remember how me and my friends used to sneak (basically breaking and entering) into the gym at my old high school to play basketball. We got caught on numerous occasions by one of the coaches and all they did was tell us that we had to leave. They could have easily called the cops, but they didn't want to see us arrested for something so minor. It's something I still appreciate to this day because some arrests could have changed the trajectory of all of our lives for the worst.

Something I've been happy to see since I've been an

adult is other coaches who I know personally that have a passion to be positive role models/mentors for kids who were like me.

Coach Malcolm Sanders of Charlotte, North Carolina has coached NBA players Steph and Seth Curry during their youth playing days with the Charlotte STARS, but he has mentored so many other kids that go unnoticed. He treats all of the kids the same way he did Steph and Seth. He has treated all of those kids like they were his own kids, a common theme with the other coaches I will be mentioning. I met Malcolm many years ago through Brian (Brian played with Dell Curry with the original Charlotte Hornets team) and I have seen all the work he does with youth in Charlotte.

Coach Dan Prete who coaches at Bishop Walsh high school became a friend of mine while he was coaching at

SPORTS HEAVEN

Montrose Christian School where he coached Kevin Durant among many other College & NBA players. I have seen him treat all of his players like he does his own sons, showing them how to become productive men. He is like "a brother from another mother" to me and has assisted me with so many things in life. He is definitely the type of person you want coaching your kids.

The last guy I want (although there are MANY MORE) to mention is Coach Malcolm Battle who used to be the Head Coach at Cesar Chavez Charter School in Washington D.C. I used to be a Physical Education teacher at that school and there were a lot of tough inner city kids who attended there. I loved my time there because it felt like I was really making a difference with some of those kids and I understood some of what they were going through. Coach Battle was a hard-nosed disciplined coach on his players but other than Coach Prete I have never seen a coach personally take care of players like he did. Food, clothes, helping kids with transportation, finding colleges for kids, whatever it took to assist them he did.

The best part about all of those guys is that there aren't any ulterior motives like some coaches have, they really want the best for their players.

I believe almost all of the successful players in every sport can attest to having a mentor/guidance/role model(s) who played a huge part in their success. Even more so, kids who are like the kid I was NEED a good mentor/guidance/role model(s) because it will help them on their journey of overcoming what they're missing.

As a kid I had some peers such as Brian and Tony who made me want to do better. I also had some coaches and

SPORTS HEAVEN

other adults who provided me with some guidance after my father passed. I look back at all the mentors/role models that I had and they played a major part in the positive way I look at life.

SPORTS HEAVEN

My brother Durrell playing in a game at Creswell High School in 1983 when the shorts were extra short. He was a very good player and that motivated me to be better or just as good.

SPORTS HEAVEN

My friend Tony Midgett (in the white jersey) his freshman year at the University of Akron. This guy made me better every summer during our teenage years and I learned a lot about playing point guard from him.

SPORTS HEAVEN

My friend Brian Rowsom's rookie card with the Charlotte Hornets. He was the first to show us that we still could make it big coming from our small town.

SPORTS HEAVEN

Coach Malcolm Sanders with Steph and Seth Curry. Like most of the coaches I know he understands it's bigger than sports.

SPORTS HEAVEN

Coach Dan Prete who has coached many college and pro basketball players. He's been a great friend for a long time.

SPORTS HEAVEN

Nate "Tiny" Archibald and me at my Basketball Exposure Event at Tarboro High School in 2001. He came and gave a great speech to the players that day.

SPORTS HEAVEN

Chapter 8: Proper Perspective

"After losing my dad, there weren't any pressure situations in sports that could bother me"

Over the years a lot of people have made fun of an Allen Iverson press conference talking about practice but I knew what he was trying to convey as soon as I saw it. Allen never said that he hated practice as a lot of people have alluded. Plus with the way veteran players are given days off to rest I thought the topic was a mute one.

There was something else going on in Allen's life that the media didn't report as much as the rant. That is the fact that Allen had lost a good friend of his. If that had been reported I think most people would have understood that Allen wasn't dismissing the importance of practice.

SPORTS HEAVEN

Allen Iverson has always been one of my favorite players and it has a lot to do with the fact that our games were similar. I also respected him and how he rose above his circumstances from his childhood and was able to make his dreams of becoming an NBA player a reality.

In the grand scheme of things sports is just a game and that is something that some people just don't get. Losing my father at age 6 made me realize that not much could get worse than that.

When I was playing little league baseball and we were playing for the league championship, the game was very tight. My team was actually losing by 1 going into the bottom of the 9th inning. I remember thinking "this is fun, this is how it supposed to be" but I also remember looking at a teammate and he was actually scared (plus shaking). At first I thought maybe he was getting sick but then I realized he was nervous because of the pressure of the moment. The funny part is I wasn't as good a hitter as some of my friends but I was looking forward to trying to hit the ball and get on base. I was the 3rd batter that inning and was on deck with no outs and one man on base. My cousin Carl hit a 2 run homerun for us to win the game. My first thought was elation of course but then my next thought was "Dang, I wonder if I could have gotten a hit?!"

That was my first experience with what people in sports call "clutch moments" or "pressure cookers." I understand why they look at those moments the way they do because they are intense but they are not important in the big picture of life. I know Allen Iverson was trying to say that "I can't believe we're here talking about practice when there are some things that are more important." Having that Proper

SPORTS HEAVEN

Perspective can put sports in its proper place and that's how it was for me.

I had many more "clutch" moments playing basketball and coaching it but I have enjoyed them all. Of course I haven't won them all but I have moved on from them regardless of the outcome. Sports has made me realize that you can lose, but learn from that loss in order to win in the future.

A perfect example of how I use Proper Perspective when coaching is whenever my team is losing by 10 or more points I never say "Ok we're down by 10 points." I say "Ok we need 5 baskets." That's not even take into consideration of the three point shot if we were able to utilize it. The 5 baskets sound a lot better than the 10 points and having a positive perception is important when you're losing.

SPORTS HEAVEN

It's the same way in life when things aren't going well for you. You don't want to hear how much you need to turn things around (it's obvious) so it's better to hear positive things to encourage you to want to turn things around.

My family has endured a great deal of tragedy and a lot of it happened during my childhood. Before my father died I had lost my Uncle Kenneth (who was in high school at that time) and cousin Jamal (who was only 4) to some horrific events. Jamal died in 1973, Kenneth in 1974, and my father in 1976. I was 3, 4, and 6 during their deaths and didn't understand how their deaths affected me until I was older.

I NEVER felt pressure in a basketball game because it wasn't REALLY life or death to miss a game winning free throw or shot. I learned about real death as a kid so I didn't understand the big deal about feeling pressure in sports. I

SPORTS HEAVEN

missed a game winning shot versus Plymouth High School (now Washington County High School) on November 23, 1987 and lived to talk about it. Now before you think I have one incredible memory, I have a memory book which has my Senior Year Basketball schedule in it so that's how I found the date.

But I remembered the game and exactly where I missed the game winning shot. I'll never forget that game but I didn't feel any pressure taking the last shot because I wouldn't shoot if I didn't believe it was going in. I had many other game winning opportunities that year and came out on the winning side on MOST of them.

My loved ones deaths made me look at sports and other trivial areas of life for what they really are. Some athletes have to train themselves how to handle the so called

SPORTS HEAVEN

"pressure situations" but it was always easy for me.

Coach Battle used to coach kids who were shot at, been shot, or seen someone get shot. You think those kids were nervous going to any gyms to play basketball?

Basketball was an escape or a haven for most of those players so they looked forward to playing the game any and everywhere. They realized because of their reality that basketball is only a game when you put it in its proper place. After losing my dad, there weren't any pressure situations in sports that could bother me.

SPORTS HEAVEN

My baseball trophies from my little league playing days. My first time playing organized sports and learning that "it's just a game."

SPORTS HEAVEN

My sophomore year of high school in a game against Mattamuskeet High school. That year provided a valuable lesson to me about the importance of education that you will learn about in the next chapter.

Chapter 7: Educational Attainment

"I'm glad you're good at basketball but you'll need your education"

I'm sure many athletes have heard this and many have probably disregarded it like I use to. I have always thought of myself as a somewhat intelligent person but school was never first on my list of priorities. Growing up watching sports, the media never emphasized the fact that a lot of those professional athletes were educated men.

It wasn't until high school that I learned how important education was because if you were failing your classes you couldn't participate in sports. One of the most painful experiences of my life was failing off the basketball team my sophomore year of high school because I failed a class during the first semester. That one class changed my outlook a great deal and even though it was a very painful moment, I am thankful for the lessons I learned from that experience.

On the court I was having a very good year averaging over 20 points and over 7 assists a game on the junior varsity team. The varsity coach had already told me that he was planning on moving me up to varsity at the end of the season for the conference and state tournament. He had actually wanted to move a couple of us up before the season started but I wanted to play JV because I thought that playing on that level and getting a chance to improve my game was a lot better than coming off the bench on the varsity.

Our varsity basketball team was very good and we had a player named Danny Moore who was one of the best scorers I have ever seen in my life. I remember at the beginning of the

SPORTS HEAVEN

season when Coach Jones called me, my friend Neil, and my uncle Andre (yes I played with my uncle) in his office. He said "I'm going to move one, maybe two of you guys up to varsity."

Well, he moved Neil up and he was the perfect fit for that team because he wasn't the type of player who needed to score. Me on the other hand, I loved playing an all-around game but scoring was number one for me.

When the mid-term grades came out in January I failed a typing class and I knew that meant trouble. I told the coach about it before I even told my mom and we went to the teacher to see if there was something I could do to bring the grade up because I was literally two points away from a grade of a C. She said I could take a test over or do some extra credit and that should help me.

So now we have a solution and everything is going to

be fine. Wrong!! I didn't feel good about the solution. For one I didn't like the teacher and the second thing is something felt wrong about me getting a second chance at something I knew I could have done better in the first time, especially when all it took was my best effort. I decided not to take the test over or do any extra credit.

As much as it hurt me not to play basketball, the pain of it all allowed me to ensure myself that it would never happen again. The worst part of it all is I went with the team during the state playoffs and watched them lose a game in double overtime to our cross-town rival Columbia High School.

We could have won the game if we had made some critical free throws down the stretch and that was something I prided myself on was making free throws "in the clutch." I still have the newspaper clipping from that game in my memory

SPORTS HEAVEN

book and it's a reminder of what I went through that year.

In the area of Eastern North Carolina where I grew up I have seen a lot of talented athletes who definitely had the potential to play their sports on the highest level, but didn't have the grades or test scores to compete in college. It's a story that's all too common in a lot of communities where education is not valued like it should be.

I started doing basketball exposure camps in my area back in 2000 because I wanted to help as many kids as I could get opportunities to be seen by college coaches. I had so many talented players come through those camps but some just weren't ready for college academically.

I also know that each individual learns differently and we shouldn't expect all students to get high grades or high test scores, but I can say that having to pass my classes in order to play basketball made me more aware about the importance of education.

A prime example of that is how my basketball recruiting process played out for me in high school. After having a pretty good senior year in basketball I was trying to see if I could get a Division 1 basketball scholarship. After the basketball season had ended that year I only had one offer and it was from a junior college. So I contacted a couple of colleges such as Towson State and Campbell University on my own to gauge their interest. Both schools were interested but wanted to know what my score was on the SAT.

It was March of my senior year in high school and I hadn't even taken the SAT yet. That shows how much thought I had put into the idea of going to college until that particular point and time. So I went and took the SAT without even

SPORTS HEAVEN

studying for it, HOPING to get the required score of 700 that was required for Division 1 student athletes to earn a scholarship to play their first year of college.

The rule was called Proposition 48 and there were some prominent coaches such as John Thompson (who actually protested Prop 42 a couple of years later) at Georgetown University who were against it because they felt the test was biased. Well I scored 680 and that meant I couldn't receive a Division 1 basketball scholarship to play my freshman year of college.

Coach Ron Lievense who was an assistant coach at Campbell University still wanted to help me out by sending me to play for his dad in Minnesota at Normandale Community College. I made the decision to go to Clinton Junior College where I didn't stay long and my college basketball career didn't go as I had planned it.

And for those of you who may be wondering, the SAT was completely different in 1988 then what it is right now. At that time you only had Math and Critical Reading with average scores being about 900 with a maximum of 1600.

The argument at that time was that the Proposition 48 rule would have an adverse effect on minority students because of the test bias. I would agree that the test is and was biased but for different reasons then what most of the people were stating then.

I don't think it's biased because of one's ethnicity but I think it's biased based on the education someone gets and probably the things some students are exposed to in their environments. I remember thinking when I was taking the test there were some words on the critical reading section that I had not seen or understood what they meant because they were not used in my environment.

A couple of the reasons that people argue for the test is that they believe it will show a student's readiness for college and a student's ability to do college level work. I'm sure I'm not the only person who has seen MANY people who do well on these tests not finish college and MANY people who don't do well on these tests finish college.

I received a Bachelor's degree in Sociology and a Masters in Sports Management, my SAT scores didn't matter at all in me achieving those but my perseverance did. I went through so many different things in life to achieve those degrees and my SAT test score didn't matter.

I think education is more than just going to school but also doing the necessary things to improve yourself. I didn't have to go to school to write this book but I had to get educated enough to tell my story and sports was the main reason I was motivated to do so.

One fact I have to mention is I became more interested in math from watching sports and wanted to learn more about math because of sports. I was watching a game once and the announcer kept saying the running back averaged 5 yards a carry during the game. I thought "how did he know that because he finished the game with 125 yards and carried the ball 25 times??"

Then one of my uncles told me that you divide the yards by the number of times he carried the ball. Okay so 125 divided by 25 is 5, so now I thought I was a genius because I did the same thing with the wide receivers. If Lynn Swann caught 8 passes for 110 yards then he averaged 13.7(basically

SPORTS HEAVEN

14) yards a catch.

So that's how it went in other sports as well, I started understanding how someone could average a certain number of points, assists, rebounds, steals, and all the other statistics athletes achieve. So sports was vital in my educational attainment because there are some areas in sports such as statistics that require you to have a basic knowledge of math.

It happened with other subjects as well, I don't like history but I love sports history and I enjoy reading about it. Learning about the volume and area of an object bored me but I was intrigued to know that three regulation size basketballs can fit in a hoop at the same time. I can't recall my teachers or professors talking about air but I know that the altitude in Denver effects players who play there, especially visiting team's players who aren't used to it.

SPORTS HEAVEN

My interest in education and learning was enhanced because of my involvement with sports and it made me smarter or more educated because of that. I realized that I couldn't separate the two IF I wanted to be the best person I could be. I'm glad I was listening when my grandmother Beulah told me "I'm glad you're good at basketball but you'll need your education."

SPORTS HEAVEN

My high school graduation day with friends I had been in class with since kindergarten. That's me second from the far right.

Chapter 6: Positive Reinforcement

"Confidence is born from the belief of others in you as well as your own belief"

We all love to be praised or given a positive comment about something we have done. In the sports world the simple words of a coach or teammate saying "good job" resonates deeply in a player's mindset. There's a reason why most teams play better at home than away, the love you get from the home crowd causes you to have increased adrenaline to play harder.

I also enjoyed playing away games too, especially when the crowd was hostile but that's because I enjoyed the sound of silence when you started beating their team. Yeah, sometimes in sports you have to be the bad guy.

SPORTS HEAVEN

However, nothing was like playing in front of your home crowd and the support they gave. So when you're going through some hard times in life, competing in sports and getting positive feedback from coaches, teammates, and fans can do a lot to pick up your psyche. "Great shot", "good pass", "smart play", "nice defense", and "way to hustle" are some comments that echo in my memory bank and I especially enjoyed hearing them when I was down mentally.

In any positive sports environment those are the things you will hear on a daily basis and most coaches know that those comments produce a winning attitude amongst your players. There will be bad things to happen on the sports field as well, but the idea is to create an atmosphere where there is more praise than criticism.

I could have been having a bad day at school, but when

SPORTS HEAVEN

I went on that baseball field or basketball court and heard positive praise from my coaches or teammates, life just felt so much better. Learning that fact also helped me as a teacher and a coach, I would also add as a father.

I know the best way to be critical of someone is to put it in the nicest way as possible.

Saying "you're smarter than that" is a whole lot better than saying "that was a dumb play." I would especially implore all coaches and teachers to take this approach when dealing with kids who have lost the presence of a parent. Most kids like that are extra sensitive to criticism that is not constructive.

I had my moments with certain coaches and teachers who didn't seem to know the power of Positive Reinforcement. I've never taken too kindly to instruction or coaching that was borderline belittling to me even if the teacher or coach had good intentions, and I grew up in an era where harsh tones from elders or leaders was the norm.

One of the main reasons I wanted to grow up was so certain people couldn't talk to me in a way I found demeaning. My big plan was "I'm going to show that ……. something when I get older." It sounds funny, but it's so true.

The best way in my opinion to deal with many rebellious kids is to tell them they "can do better" and after hearing that constantly eventually they will probably do better. I was lucky to have a lot of caring family members, friends, **some** teachers, and **some** coaches who told me "You can do it!" which gave me the confidence to follow my goals.

My high school basketball career is a perfect example of getting positive reinforcement at the right moment from the right person. I had a very good senior year in basketball: I averaged 18 points per game, 9 assists per game, made the Tobacco Belt All-Conference team, The Washington Daily Newspaper All-Area team, and was honorable mention All-State.

    I didn't believe I could play basketball on the college level until our assistant coach Roy Prince who had just moved to Creswell and had been around college players before that, told me after a game against Plymouth High (which was a class 3A team while we were class 1A) that "Anthony you can play basketball on the highest level, you have the skills to do that."

    An ironic twist in my ability to get a college basketball scholarship is that Coach Prince is the reason I received my first offer from Clinton Junior College.

    Once my senior season was over I didn't have an offer

up to that point and that was the end of February. One day I walked into the coach's office to see Coach Prince who coached the girls' basketball team. He was on the phone with Coach H.K. Harrison of Clinton Junior College trying to see if he could get a basketball scholarship for one of the players on his girls' team.

But Coach Harrison stated that Clinton didn't have a girls' team, only a boys' team. That's when Coach Prince told him "Well I have a point guard here on the boys team that can run an offense like running water in a bucket." I remember him saying that so vividly like it was yesterday and something I'll never forget because he helped me when he wasn't even my coach.

He got the coaches address and sent him a video of my last Senior Night home game versus Aurora High School where

SPORTS HEAVEN

I had 25 points, 6 assists, and 4 steals in about 18 minutes of playing time. Coach Harrison started calling me every day after he watched the video and offered me a scholarship from day one. I signed the Letter of Intent a month later and it was a fulfilling feeling I can't describe.

The video that Coach Prince sent Coach Harrison is in my video collection, I even transferred it from VHS tape to DVD. I didn't realize it then, but most of my friends say they don't have any video from when they played in high school.

I'll watch it from time to time to see if I was as good as I thought I was and I guess I was alright. There's also a part that I like to listen to when I can hear Coach Prince's voice yelling "Anthony!" when it looked like I was about to commit a foul. Better yet it reminds me of what he did for me by giving me that positive reinforcement….

SPORTS HEAVEN

Mr. Roy Prince
Health/Physical Ed.

Coach Prince who was very instrumental in me getting my basketball scholarship to Clinton Junior College.

SPORTS HEAVEN

Me with a camper at my old high school. I believe in "passing it forward" and I love teaching kids what I learned.

Chapter 5: Faith & Character Builder

"……I was taught some life lessons in sports that I couldn't have learned elsewhere"

Whether you believe in a higher being (God, Allah, Jehovah, etc.) or not, things in life will test your resolve and character. Losing someone you love is the hardest thing in life and I had to endure that tragedy at a young age.

I've never been one to proselytize (I discovered what that word meant reading a sports book as a teenager) to anyone about my beliefs in God because I've always disliked it when someone has tried to convince me about the religion they believe in and wanted me to believe in it like them.

When you're great or good at something people will want to know how and why you did it. I think that's the

SPORTS HEAVEN

perfect opportunity to explain your faith and what you believe in. Success provides people a platform to speak about why they are successful and what they believe in.

Anyone who can relate to being down by 20 plus points in a basketball game or a large margin in any other sport and then come back to win in what looks like a miracle, knows the feeling of having faith in your athletic ability. I'm sure the best athletes can attest to feeling confident even while they're losing because they believe they're still going to win.

That happens a lot in sports when you're losing and then all of a sudden that sports lion called "momentum" starts to roar your way until you win. Sometimes you don't come back to win but the experience builds faith and character.

I've always hoped that my kids will find something that

they are passionate about and want to be good at, but I've also hoped that they wouldn't be successful at it in the beginning. Yes, it's true because something they want to be good at and are passionate about shouldn't be easily attainable.

I love my kids more than anything ever and of course I want the best for them, but I know being the best requires some work. First, anyone who's willing to work hard is going to need discipline to put the necessary time in to get better. That discipline will show your character, which most of us knows is "what you do when no one's watching."

It also means you are probably sacrificing something in order to acquire that discipline but that's another part of the process. My older kids Cameron and Bria can attest, I always tell them "Put the work in and do your best to get better at everything you do" and I add that "It's a process." My 6 year old son Chance will hear it a lot too and it's because I believe in that.

Everything I have put extreme hard work into I have gotten better at it. There are some things I don't want to get better at so I don't put any work into it at all. But I have broken many bones and suffered a lot of scars to get better at basketball.

When it comes to discussing faith I know a lot of people would like to separate anything with religious connections from sports, but that would require the majority of athletes to lose an important part of their identity. Sports is a great melting pot of religious, economic, racial, and ethnic backgrounds and that is one of the things that makes sports so great.

SPORTS HEAVEN

In basketball you can have a starting five of the following religions: A Christian point guard, a Jewish shooting guard, a small forward who is Hindu, a Muslim center, and a power forward who is a Jehovah's Witness. A lot can be learned from sports and the way athletes integrate for the better good of the team.

I have met athletes from many diverse backgrounds and it has allowed me to look at things from different perspectives. Too many times WE are guilty of not accepting someone's views or beliefs because they are different from our own. IF you are willing, sports can teach anyone about tolerance and acceptance which enhances character.

Of course there are racists, sexists, and all of those other negative attitudes that exist in sports like society but in my opinion they're the minority. Sports is a place where you can grow up being taught that a particular group of people are labeled to be a certain way and then when you get to know those group of people, you realize that label is far from the truth.

Sports is a global connector and is a wonderful way for the world to grow together. I have Christian friends, Muslim friends, Jewish friends, and friends from other religions. I have learned so much from them all and I don't understand why the world is so divisive when it comes to religions.

I would add that I don't understand why some people are like that with a person's race or sex as well. I'm not colorblind, but I measure a person by who they are and not what race or sex they are, that seems so ignorant to me.

As for my own faith I believe in a higher spiritual power but I don't consider myself to be just a Christian, Muslim, or

SPORTS HEAVEN

Jewish but I consider myself to be a combination of all religions that believe in what I do and do THEIR BEST to love everyone deserving of it.

Two of my favorite athletes were Muhamad Ali and Kareem Abdul-Jabbar who are both Muslim. I learned a lot about their religion because of them and I have always respected the way they carried themselves. They brought attention to their religion because of their greatness in their particular sports, but they both were also socially conscious.

Another important aspect about sports and character building is that you learn how to win and lose. I hate losing and if you're a competitive person then that's part of who you are. The term "sore loser" applies to individuals who don't know how to show good sportsmanship after they lose.

When I first started playing baseball I remember I used

to throw bats after striking out or not wanting to shake hands with the opposing team after we lost, even though we were supposed to do that. Then I started watching better players who would strike out and their response was a lot calmer than mine so I took that to heart. I thought "if those guys can be calm after striking out then I can too" so I got better with that. I still hated striking out, but that was a part of the process of getting better.

Losing is one of the hardest things to deal with in sports, but it really does prepare you for winning. It makes you realize that you have to get better in whatever areas the other team (or individual for individual sports) is better. The only way to become your best is to get better in the areas you're weak in, it sounds cliché but it's all truth.

That truth carries over to your personal life as well

SPORTS HEAVEN

where we all desire to be our best version of ourselves. Sports has been an invaluable teacher with my faith and character, I was taught some life lessons in sports that I couldn't have learned elsewhere.

SPORTS HEAVEN

Some of the players I coached at a private school in Northern Virginia. A lot of different cultures and race of kids, I learned from them just as much as they learned from me.

Chapter 4: Financial Attainment & Financial Literacy

"Extraordinary talent can be an equalizer when it comes to money"

Most of the time when there is a parent missing, or not involved in a kids life there will be some financial strain in that child's life. After my father died I remember things started changing for us financially but I didn't notice it much until many years later. My mother remarried so things were fine until they got a divorce when I was in 8th grade, then things really went downhill.

Most sports require the parents to pay some type of money such as fees for uniforms and the other fees that an organization has to cover such as paying officials. I got my first taste playing little league baseball and what it meant when

SPORTS HEAVEN

you are good at a sport, then someone was willing to pay those fees for your parents.

I had a couple of older friends who were really good at baseball, but their parents weren't in the best shape financially either. They told me how they didn't pay the fees or anything else for that matter. I wanted to play baseball, but I wasn't as good as those guys and I knew my mom wouldn't want to pay the fees that came with it.

Access is an amazing thing, whether we're talking about access to money, food, a good education or whatever you can think of, having access can provide opportunities. So I had access to family (specifically my uncle Andre) and friends (Vic and Calvin Blount, Darnell Norman, Dion Spencer) who could help me get better at baseball so I utilized them to the fullest extent. I practiced with those guys a whole lot and we

SPORTS HEAVEN

played baseball around the house almost every day. I got better and found a team that needed me.

I didn't even have to tell the coach that my mom couldn't pay the fees because I think he knew that already, since everyone knew everyone in the small town I grew up in. The coach even had a younger brother in my class who knew me and he was the one who invited me to play with their team. I didn't have to pay anything and there were times when the coach would come pick us up to make sure we made it to the games on time.

That was when I realized that my athletic ability could pay dividends and I mean literally. I was 13 years old and had already started working on farms with one of my uncles, so I knew the value of hard work. However, working on a farm wasn't something I wanted to do in the future. I didn't like it

SPORTS HEAVEN

because it felt like Slave labor even though we were getting paid.

My entire mindset changed once I realized that sports could change my financial position in life. I wasn't thinking about long term things such as professional sports but we'll get to that later.

I played baseball because all of my friends around me did but basketball was my favorite sport. It was because of basketball that I realized the difference between amateur athletes and professional athletes. I was watching an NBA game and the announcers started talking about how the Lakers were planning to sign Magic Johnson to a 25 year contract for 1 Million dollars per year.

I didn't even know that the players were getting paid to play, I thought they were doing it for fun like we were as kids. It was like a light bulb came on in my head and said "Man if you can be good at this you can be rich from JUST playing basketball."

That wasn't the most important thing I learned about financial attainment when I realized they got paid, it was the other aspects of finances that enhanced my financial literacy.

It was the terms such as **salaries, expenses, per diem, team payroll, roster bonus, salary cap, contract, contract extension, revenue sharing, operating expenses, investments, gate receipts, and return on investments.**

I had never heard anyone around me talking about those things, and I don't even remember hearing about them on TV or elsewhere. Even my time in high school most of those terms weren't used so I found out what they were from sports.

SPORTS HEAVEN

When I started my Next Level Sports Management business in 2000, having an understanding of those terms came in handy because I had to know most of those things in order to operate my business efficiently. There probably are many other athletes who hadn't heard some of those terms until they started participating in sports.

Those terms became important to me because I had to understand what a contract is even if it's a contract for a job or cable service (drop your service too soon and expect some added fees right?). I believe what comes to mind when most people think about professional athletes is the millions of dollars that most of them make, but there are some other financial advantages that come with it.

One advantage is, athletes meet successful individuals from various parts of society who can help them learn more about other opportunities they can take advantage of during their off time and after their playing careers are done. I didn't play professional basketball, but basketball has allowed me to meet so many successful people from other walks of life. CEOs, doctors, lawyers, money managers, various entrepreneurs, high ranking military officials, I could make a huge list of successful people I have met and become acquainted with. Some I consider friends from meeting them through basketball.

Most of those people are willing to offer their expertise or knowledge in how to manage money, and that is something I have been blessed to experience. I didn't grow up with people educating me about money and that's the case with most of us because financial literacy isn't taught in most classrooms.

SPORTS HEAVEN

I knew my grandmother Beulah (my dad's mom) and my grandmother Mary Elizabeth (my mom's mom) always SEEMED to have money because they used to give me money quite a bit. Then I realized as I grew older that was because they knew how to manage what they had.

My grandmother Beulah even gave us a small allowance on the weekends when we were staying with her. On Sundays the change was meant for the offering plate at church, and the fact she trusted us to put it in (and not keep it) is perplexing to me.

Neither of them was rich or had a lot in regards to material things, but they had an innate ability of "putting money to the side", their actual words for saving. I didn't know what they meant by that until I became an adult and started doing it myself.

SPORTS HEAVEN

If you follow sports at all I am sure you hear the horror stories of professional athletes going broke after their playing careers have ended, but there are some positive stories as well. There many athletes who don't make it to the professional level in sports but have become productive and successful citizens in other professions.

As the case with my educational attainment, basketball provided me with a means to enhance my financial attainment. I didn't have to wonder how my mom was going to get money to pay for me to go to college because of my basketball scholarship.

There are many former and current athletes out there who never would have attended or attend college if it wasn't for them playing sports because their financial circumstances wouldn't have allowed it. Just think about what would happen

SPORTS HEAVEN

if you took away the athletic scholarships that so many kids relied on in the past and rely on right now.

Think about all the great athletes who have used college athletics to improve their lives. I was one of those kids who needed that athletic scholarship. Even though my college playing career didn't go like I wanted it to, I was still able to get into college and get that opportunity to improve myself. I wouldn't have gone to college if it wasn't for basketball and I knew that.

I learned even more about finances after I stopped playing college basketball because I had to find another way to pay for school, but it was a necessary lesson. That's when I learned about loans, promissory notes, deferred payments, and interest rates. Since I was an independent student which meant I was paying my own way through college, I had to get an understanding of those terms.

When you hear those horror stories about professional athletes going broke, it's because MOST of them likely didn't have the financial training to become financial literate. Additionally, many athletes are young when they get all of that money. Combine that with no financial training and you have a recipe for money management disaster.

It can be said there are different reasons at fault. The first is our educational system doesn't teach financial literacy. Another is when you come from a household where parents aren't financially sound then you probably won't be either.

We all have likely heard someone say "If I had all that money I would never go broke" (I'm sure I've said it once or twice) or something along those lines. But I think that's easier said than done, especially when most of the people who say that aren't financial literate themselves.

I don't care how much money you make if you don't understand the concept of spending less than you make you'll go broke.

My best times in sports were when I was playing for fun and doing it because I loved it, but once I knew it could change my life financially then I was even more motivated.

I hear the critics who say there are communities who place too much emphasis on sports. That there should be more emphasis on kids in those communities focusing on other professions, because the odds of playing collegiately and professionally are so small. However, having athletic ability or any ability that can teach you about financial independence and other financial lessons is invaluable.

That athletic ability also allows them to get a college

scholarship to pay for school and get an opportunity to improve their circumstances.

Why do you think most kids dream of playing professional sports? Yes, the money they hear about these athletes making are enough to make anybody want to be a professional athlete. That's when kids becomes curious about the financial aspects of making money when they see athletes they look up to making huge sums of it.

I didn't have access to research financial information as easily as kids do now because technology (specifically the internet) wasn't available the way it is now. Kids now can look up various details such as **signing bonuses, league pension plans, pay schedule (yes some professional athletes get paid every two weeks like normal people), players unions, contract incentives(similar to commissions),** and other issues that deal with player's money. Many of those terms and issues are relevant to other professions and not just specific to professional athletes. Since most athletes won't play professional sports, it helps that they understand certain concepts so they can maximize their earnings elsewhere.

Sports has impacted my thinking in regards to economics even at this very moment in my life because I have started learning more about the aspects of owning a professional sports team along with the dynamics of money involved in every area of sports. As great as sports has been to me in regards to financial incentives, I do have some grievances in regards to how the system is designed in some areas (much like society).

The first thing is when I took Sports Finance while I was getting my Master's Degree I learned more in those eight

SPORTS HEAVEN

weeks about the financing involved in sports than I ever had at any time during my life. The way that some NFL stadiums and NBA arenas are financed by public money really caught my attention, because I used to think that the owners were always paying for those things with their own money.

Next there are the sponsorships by major companies, the TV deals, merchandise sales, and so many other things that I'm sure the average sports fans are not aware of. I also believe that most of the pro athletes involved aren't aware of the intricate financial aspects either, because in my opinion they should have started their own league or at the very least have some teams of their own once they retire.

Most players after they retire don't even get an opportunity to be a part of any of the professional team's management. They can dedicate many years playing for a team, but once their careers are over it's basically "good luck with the rest of your life."

The critics and pessimists will claim that players can't have their own league or have more input in management decisions as if we don't have professional sports teams who aren't owned by fans already. Research the Green Bay Packers and some pro soccer teams as examples.

Every time I see these players going back and forth with these owners about issues in their respective collective bargaining agreements I think to myself "you wouldn't have these problems if you were a part of the ownership structure."

I also believe that professional athletes from all the major professional leagues should start their own banks with some of the money they're being paid. Imagine if most of the pro athletes from the NBA, NFL, MLB, and NHL formed their own banks. That is billions of dollars from those leagues alone and I think other professional athletes along with fans would want to become members of the player's banks because of the affiliation.

It may sound like a radical or revolutionary idea but it's one that I think can be done with success if those players would commit to it. Hopefully some players with some leverage will decide to try it and see what happens.

The same issues apply in major college sports where the players at these colleges are making the money for those schools but they don't get to enjoy the financial rewards like the people in charge do.

It all has to change in order for some of those athletes to be able to change the financial trajectories of their lives. If their coaches and colleges they play for are getting wealthy, they should have the ability to do so as well.

So if THE MASSES (in this case the athletes) of people started using their leverage to activate change then we would get it, this isn't anything new that hasn't been done or said before.

My love for sports is the reason I research financial elements that effect all of society and it is the reason I have a better understanding about financial attainment. A lot of athletes become financially literate because extraordinary talent can be an equalizer when it comes to money.

SPORTS HEAVEN

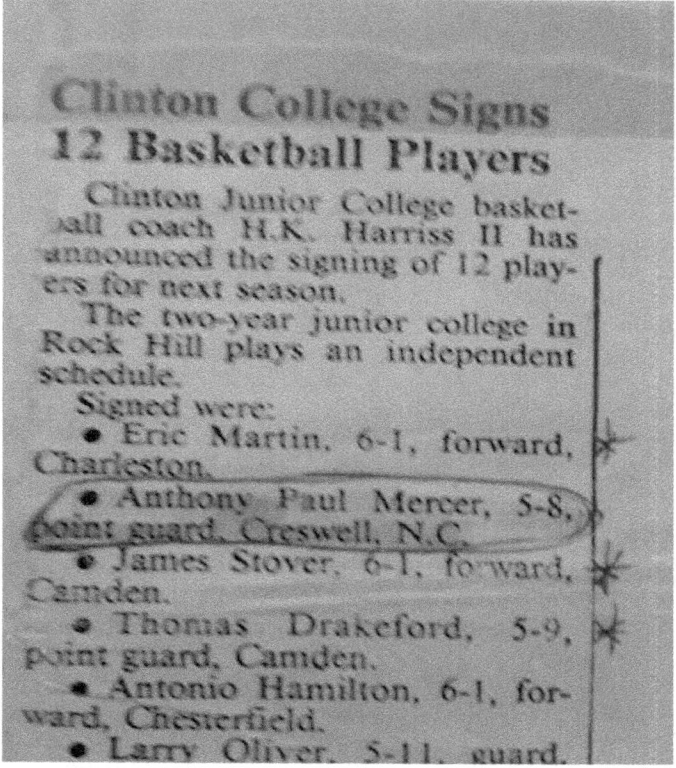

A newspaper clipping showing my signing to Clinton Junior College. Getting that scholarship paved the way for me to get into college and not worry about how to pay for it.

SPORTS HEAVEN

Me at a basketball camp with my friend Jeff Lubitz who has a wealth of experience in the financial and business sectors. I met Jeff after I was coaching his daughter Shayna at a Wizards basketball camp. He has given me financial advice, sponsored kids at my camps, and even bought copies of this book before it was finished to give away to kids.

SPORTS HEAVEN

Me with Dallas Mavericks owner Mark Cuban in 2017. I have always admired his business acumen, but the way he provided help to his former player Delonte West is more admirable.

Chapter 3: Examples of Others in Similar Pain

"There are many people who have experienced the same pain"

Throughout my time being involved in sports I have come across many athletes, who have experienced the same pain I did after losing my dad. As I mentioned in the beginning of the book, some of those individuals had living parents who weren't involved in their lives for one reason or another. Some even had both parents in the household but were still missing that parental guidance.

I used to think that I was alone in what I was going through, but my life in sports has made me realize that there are MILLIONS of people going through what I did. I have read about and met so many other athletes who went through the

SPORTS HEAVEN

same pain that I did.

My plan with this chapter was to interview as many professional athletes, coaches, executives, and others who have experienced traumatic losses. But trying to get into contact with the people I wanted to interview was very tough, especially during a pandemic. Hopefully, in the future I'll be able to get some of those individuals involved with my basketball camps/book events.

I decided to do this chapter without them and just mention some of those individuals who have had similar experiences. I was able to conduct a phone interview with one professional athlete and that was WNBA player Ta'Shauna "Sugar" Rodgers. She is a current WNBA player with the Las Vegas Aces and played collegiately at Georgetown University for my friend Coach Keith Brown. Keith was the person responsible for me getting the interview with Sugar because they are still very close.

"Sugar" lost both of her parents during her early teenage years but did not let that or any other of life's struggles keep her from being a success on the basketball court and in life. If you haven't heard of Sugar's story please research her because it is heartbreaking and heartwarming at the same time.

When I interviewed her the first thing I wanted her to know is how we were similar in losing a parent at a young age and used sports to deal with our pain. I asked her if basketball was like therapy for her after her mom passed and she said "It was like an escape from reality, a safe haven from all the things I was going through in my life. Just a way to enjoy being a kid." She explained to me how "Basketball saved my life, I don't know what I would have done without it" and a similar notion that I had that "pressure is worrying about where your next meal is coming from, I never felt pressure from playing basketball."

We discussed many other aspects of how basketball was important in her development such as getting the basketball scholarship to Georgetown University, the mentorships from her cousin Keda and older niece Kakie, and the financial benefits of being a professional player.

She stressed that "Basketball prepared me for the real world and showed me how to deal with so many things that are reality, I have learned how to adapt and interact in any environment with various types of people."

I enjoyed interviewing her, and to see how positive she is reminded me that even after being dealt with tragedy in our

SPORTS HEAVEN

lives we can go forward the best that we can.

When I was younger(especially in high school) I thought I was the only person going through the loss of a parent because all of my friends were in two parent households or both of their parents were involved in their lives. Now I have to give props to my deceased stepfather Charles Brickhouse because he did a good job as a dad before him and my mom separated while I was in middle school. We were also very close even after that, but there was nothing he could do to replace my biological father because my dad spent a lot of time with us during the years we had him alive.

Since there wasn't a lot of technology like there is now I didn't know about the backgrounds of the athletes so I didn't learn about some of them until I got older. Hall of fame NBA players such as Bill Russell, Julius "Dr. J" Erving, Isiah Thomas,

SPORTS HEAVEN

Larry Bird, and Charles Barkley all grew up with the loss of a parent or a parent not involved in their lives. And those are just a few players I found out about because I enjoyed watching those players play.

When I got involved with conducting basketball camps in 1998 is when I began meeting players who had similar experiences as mine. Sports media outlets seemed to start discussing athletes like that on various platforms as well. I suppose a lot of people like seeing the "feel good" stories of athletes overcoming obstacles in that manner, so now it's normal to hear the same story from different athletes many times over.

I have a problem with the way the narrative is sometimes portrayed because the pain the athletes went through becomes normalized. As if they're not dealing with the hurt any longer. It's a lifetime pain and many athletes haven't been able to deal with it in a positive way. There are grown men and women right now dealing with personal issues because of the loss of a parent, abandonment by a parent(s), a parent who has been jailed, or a parent(s) who was physically present but emotionally absent in their lives.

One of the first players I met at a basketball camp where I was coaching, who had lost his dad at a young age like I did was Nolan Smith. Nolan was in high school at the time and helping out at Todd Bozeman's basketball camp. Nolan was a highly recruited college basketball prospect along with some other great high school players there such as Mike Beasley, Ty Lawson, and Navorro Bowman. There were even a couple of younger kids at that camp now who are playing in the NBA. One thing I love about teaching basketball camps is I get to see kids at the beginning of their basketball journey and watch them develop.

Nolan's dad was Derek Smith who starred at the University of Louisville where he won a national championship and played in the NBA. Nolan eventually went to Duke University where he had a good college career and won a national championship like his dad. He was drafted by the Portland Trailblazers in the 2011 and played overseas for a couple of years before going into coaching back at Duke.

I noticed that Nolan wasn't the only player at Duke that had lost a parent at a young age. Kyrie Irving, Jahlil Okafor, and Quinn Cook were players who went through similar experiences. Although I sometimes root for the Tar Heels, I wanted all of those guys to do well because they had experienced the same kind of tragedy that I had. I still follow their careers now and wish them the best.

I have done basketball camps with Carmelo Anthony and John Wall who are two of the nicest guys you'll ever want to meet. They're very competitive on the court which has made them both All-Stars many times over, but they are actively involved in their communities. They too have lost a parent (their dads) at a young age.

I actually told John's mom Frances (who recently passed in December 2019) years ago at one of his camps that I was going to write this book and do camps for kids who have been affected by loss like we have. She told me it was a great idea and that it would help many kids.

John is a good man with the heart of gold because he has done so many unselfish things for people that go unnoticed or isn't publicized.

SPORTS HEAVEN

For example, I had a former middle school basketball player of mine's named Justin who was going through cancer treatments for Ewing's Sarcoma. I wanted to do something special for him after he came from Philadelphia for one of his treatments. I texted John after not getting a response from one of the Wizard's assistant coaches and a sports agent I knew, about getting tickets for me and Justin to that night's Wizards game.

Now this was only about 3 hours before tip-off so I felt bad about texting him because I knew he was getting ready for the game. All his text said was "What's your first name Coach?" and "I got you."

Not only did John get us tickets but he brought me and Justin to the back near the locker room where he had a gift bag for Justin, plus took pictures with us. The media didn't know about it and it wasn't done for publicity, it was straight from John's heart. I appreciated what John had done for Justin and it will always be something I'll remember.

Another one of my old campers that I keep in contact with named Max told me recently that"...as a man who also lost his father at age 7, I truly know the value of sports on my life." Often there are times when we are going through hard times in life it feels like we're the only one going through it. It helps to know that there are many others who have experienced the same pain.

SPORTS HEAVEN

John Wall with Justin and me after the Wizards game was over.

SPORTS HEAVEN

Me with Carmelo Anthony after winning The Coach of the Camp Award at his New York Camp.

SPORTS HEAVEN

Chapter 2: Self-Esteem/Self-Confidence

"I feel 100% comfortable being myself wherever I am"

When you're a kid and don't have much in terms of material things, it can make you feel inferior to your peers, which is a horrible feeling. Since we didn't have much in regards to financial means, I felt that way most of the time.

It also didn't help me that I was much shorter than most of the people my age and that was almost always the case when I played sports. To add insult to injury, my nickname is "Ant" (SHORT for Anthony). My height or lack thereof was something I heard about all the time. Mainly the questions and answers like "you're 13??! You look 10!"

Once I became good at sports those questions became

less common which helped with my self-esteem. That improved self-esteem gave me the self-awareness that I could be different and good at the same time. It allowed me to understand how to use my perceived shortcoming as an advantage.

For example, I learned that in basketball a lot of players hated guarding short players because on defense they didn't like the idea of getting in a low defensive stance for long periods of time. I was also fast, so I enjoyed running around players as soon as they got into their defensive stance. Then, when I was on defense I also knew that taller guards didn't like being guarded for 94 feet (that's full court for those who don't know) by pesky little guards like me. I took joy in playing defense that way because it was my main advantage.

As a coach I tell my players the best teams are ones

SPORTS HEAVEN

who utilize their advantages more than the other team does, similar to focusing on what you can do as opposed to what you can't. Being good at sports greatly improved my self-esteem which carried over into other areas of my life. This gave me more confidence in myself, especially in school.

When you're a kid in a learning environment such as a classroom, one of the hardest things is being in front of your classmates. Even harder than that, is being in front of your classmates and not knowing the answers to questions. Nobody wants to feel stupid or dumb and I remember that feeling when you don't have high self-esteem.

That's where the sports "classroom" is a lot better than the actual academic classroom. Most coaches promote the idea of players telling them they don't know what's going on so they (the coaches) can teach it. Show me a great coach and I'll say that coach is a great teacher. Think of the great coaches you know and find out what they say about teaching their sports.

I learned from sports that it is okay not to know how to do something, but with correct repetition you can get better. I didn't particularly like math, but my frustrations with it waned because of my higher self-esteem. I didn't "beat myself" up as much when I couldn't understand certain concepts. The idea of asking for help or telling the teacher I didn't understand something became easier for me, because that's what I had learned to do in sports.

One of my first lessons in baseball was during practice the coach explained why as a hitter you don't swing at the next pitch when the count is 3 balls and no strikes. **I thought** you should always be ready to swing at a good pitch no matter what. His and most coaches reasoning behind that is the hitter is only 1 ball away from getting awarded a walk to 1st base. Therefore the probability of striking out or hitting out is much lower than the percentage of getting on base with a walk. I'm glad I asked him because it made sense and I wasn't the only one who didn't understand the reasoning at first. But since the coach always told us to ask him questions when we didn't understand something, which is what we did.

Improving my self-esteem also allowed me to "be myself" more as a person and not try to be like my peers. I started feeling good about who I was and I didn't look for validation from others. I have seen so many people TRY to be someone other than themselves.

I remember moments before I got better self-esteem where I would do things or want things because everyone else was doing it or had it. It was the "cool" thing or "dope" thing to do, but not always the right thing. Wearing "cool" shoes that were killing my feet and giving me "corns" on the top of my toes. Throwing rocks at cars as they drove by, ok remember I grew up in the country so we had to be creative.

Once my self-esteem was at a level where I needed it to be. I became an independent thinker and it has carried me throughout the rest of my life. I care about how other people feel, but not more than how I feel.

My senior year in high school basketball I used to wear knee pads with my socks pulled up high to the knee pads. I was the only player doing it and I remember I used to get teased by fans from other teams about it. I didn't care, I used to love getting the last laugh when they realized that I could play.

SPORTS HEAVEN

I wasn't doing it to be different, I actually started doing it because I hated putting lotion on my legs before games since it would make my hands slippery. I remember how some of my teammates used to worry about having ashy legs, so they would put lotion on them. You See? Some guys are just like women when it comes to trying to look nice, even at the expense of having slippery hands on the basketball court.

Once I got comfortable wearing my socks high with the knee pads, that was the way it was for me and the hecklers didn't bother me. It's amazing the focus you acquire when you have a great deal of self-confidence in yourself.

I remember all of those times when I was practicing basketball by myself to ease my mind off of thinking about the pain of losing my dad, it seemed like I was in my own world. I couldn't hear the cars passing by or the birds chirping, all I could see was the ball going in the hoop or the ball being dribbled from right to left. That focus carried over to the games I would play in front of crowds and there were times when I felt as if I was in my own world then too.

My wife, kids, my mom or anybody who knows me will tell you that I don't hear anything when I'm doing something sports related. I can't count the number of instances someone was laughing at me and I would ask "what are you laughing at?" and they would say "you, because I was calling your name so many times and you didn't budge."

It's especially that way when I'm teaching basketball or watching a good game on TV. That focus gave me the self-confidence I needed to better myself in other things, and it all can be attributed to sports.

Throughout my life, I have been around very rich

people and very poor people. I carry myself the same in both environments because I don't believe the very rich people are any better than me and the very poor people aren't any less than me.

My self-confidence allows me to be myself and not feel the need to act like I'm someone I'm not. I take pride in that because I like authentic things and authentic people. Being good at basketball gave me the self-esteem and self-confidence I needed to be true to myself. It also helped me to love myself more.

As I mentioned earlier I was almost always the shortest player on the basketball court because basketball is made up of some extraordinary large players. I learned not to dwell on that fact and just let my skills show that I was good enough regardless.

SPORTS HEAVEN

Having a strong belief in yourself is important when going through the ups and downs (especially the downs) of life because it keeps you motivated to see things through.

I could be wrong but I believe all successful people need to have a high degree of self-confidence in order to do what they do well. I believe that whatever skills and gifts you have is the doorway to having high self-confidence. Realizing you're good at something and taking pride in it motivates you.

A part of my self-confidence is that if I have to get something done, I don't like relying on other people and I don't expect help. If I get help it's cool but I don't expect it. Losing my dad made me realize that there would be a lot of times where I would have to do things on my own.

SPORTS HEAVEN

One important skill from being a point guard in basketball that translated into my personality is being able to communicate with my teammates about plays being called and knowing where everyone is supposed to be. It's the same with a quarterback on a football team, they have to know everything about the team's offense.

Since I was a point guard it forced me to communicate with my teammates and be a leader in regards to directing what we were doing on the floor. It all helped with my self-esteem and confidence. I've never had a problem speaking my mind because of that. When I'm asked about something I'm going to give my honest opinion based on the facts I know, without being apologetic.

I know who I am, I like who I am, and I love who I am. Not even close to being perfect, but I'm confident being imperfect. It is so important to love yourself, it has been said by many people and I firmly believe that.

Sports is the one place I learned being imperfect could be a positive. For example: you could hit 40 percent of pitches thrown your way in baseball to be considered a good hitter, make 50 percent of your shots as a basketball player to be called a good shooter, and complete 60 percent of your passes as a quarterback to be a good passer.

Knowing that I wasn't expected to hit every ball in baseball or to make every shot in basketball gave me the mindset to just do my best, then see what the results were. In the academic world if you get results below 70 percent you're considered a failure and will probably be labeled as someone not that smart.

No one ever told me that there were different areas

SPORTS HEAVEN

where someone could be smart or creative, I used to think it was only in a classroom. I must admit that when I was younger I thought most professional athletes were just more athletic than normal people and then I saw an NFL playbook for the first time when I was a teenager, it looked like a foreign language.

My basketball playbook in high school was pretty simple, but in college it went up a notch and I realized then I had to "study the game" a lot more. I don't know the number of hours I have put into practicing basketball and learning about the game. But I do know that it has been enough for me to THINK that I am one of the best informed in regards to it.

Most of us go through life trying to find things we can be considered good at and when we find that thing(s) it helps us feel good about ourselves. I believe we all NEED to feel good about ourselves and love the person in the mirror more than you love anyone else. I'm not promoting the idea of being cocky or narcissistic, but I am advocating a level of self-confidence that allows you to feel satisfied about who you are. Sports gave me the insight that I feel 100% comfortable being myself wherever I am.

SPORTS HEAVEN

Me and my son Chance at a museum in New York with the statue of Muhammad Ali. No athlete had more self-confidence than Mr. Ali and is the first to call himself the GOAT (Greatest Of All Time).

SPORTS HEAVEN

Chapter 1: Being the Parent/Leader You Wanted/Advice from Me

"I am who I am because sports helped mold me into that"

As a kid I never thought about becoming a parent and even as a young adult being a parent wasn't on my list of goals for my future. What I did know is that if and when I became a father I would be as involved as humanly possible for my kids.

All the things I missed doing with my dad I wanted to do with my kids. Being a father has been the most important and best thing to happen in my life. I've ALWAYS TRIED to be the dad to my kids that I wished my father could have been had he lived long enough.

SPORTS HEAVEN

Anyone who knows me know that my kids are my number one priority and I take pride in being a good dad. As a matter of fact, I tell them all the time "You have the best dad ever" but I'm not expecting a trophy or anything. Wait, unless they give those out with some money or some other prize I'll take it.

I've learned some important traits from sports that has given me tools to be a good dad. Before my kids were born I had never changed a diaper and I hadn't even babysat my nieces or nephews. I didn't know a thing about kids, or how to take care of them but I was excited when I realized I was about to become a dad.

Now before I get into the depths of being a father, I have to address the "deadbeat" issue that is somewhat of a problem and I don't understand how someone can abandon their kid(s). I REALLY don't understand how someone who was missing that parental involvement in their own lives could do that to their kids.

Most kids only want the presence of their parents and couldn't less about how much money their parents have. Now, believe me I understand the importance of money when it comes to the comfort it provides and how it allows you some piece of mind. There have been times in my life since I've been a father where I was struggling with money (a special thanks to the court system for that) and my kids had no idea.

The lack of money didn't stop me from being their dad and doing what I'm supposed to do as their parent, NO MATTER THE SITUATION. I'm not going to speak any more on the "deadbeat" issue because it really does upset me that someone can CHOOSE to not be a part of a kid's life as their parent. They really don't ask for much. Okay, maybe they do ask for a lot of THINGS but what they NEED you can't buy it.

One thing I remembered most after my father died is all of the things I wish we were able to do together like something as simple as playing catch with a football or baseball. Wishing we could have played hoops together, go to Disney Land, go to beaches, and attend sports events. All things I have done with my kids because I missed out on them with my father.

I'm not sure what type of dad I would have been had my father lived for my whole life, but I'm sure I'm the dad I am because I didn't have him for most of it. Let that sink in, it's deep and something I can't explain.

I am very playful (I know my wife will say too much sometimes because I'm light on discipline) and patient with my kids because I understand how precious every moment is with them. I've learned having patience from sports, and this makes it easier when interacting with my children. It also reminds me that I am the adult and I'm the one they're looking at as a model.

    Kids can become discouraged when first trying sports because they may not be good at first. If you can get them to understand that there's a PROCESS to improving then most of them wouldn't give up. Most of the steps of getting better in sports is similar to helping your kids learn to walk, talk, and do other things to become independent.

    When I first started playing little league baseball that coach was the first coach I ever had. I remember how much I learned about baseball because of how patient he was with all of us. He understood that kids "clown around" a lot, that we would make mistakes, but he could discipline without being demeaning or abusive, and teach us that the game was meant to be fun.

Read those things again and notice how similar they are to what parents SHOULD BE with their kids. Those positive things have stayed with me throughout my life and were things I wanted to make sure I utilized when I became a parent, coach, or in any other leadership position.

I know there are some people who think that winning is the only thing that matters in sports, but there is more to it than that because eventually your sports career will end. In professional sports I understand winning is important but there are still other lessons to be learned even on that level.

Most people don't even get a chance to play sports on the high school level so they have to start early in terms of thinking about future career goals. Many college athletes don't play professionally so they have a couple more years to enjoy before they have to think about another career.

Then you have professional athletes where most of them have short pro careers or even if they play for a long period of time they're still relatively young when they retire. Hopefully, whenever their athletic career ends they will take the lessons they learned from sports and apply them wherever necessary to their lives.

In sports you get to be around different personalities and you get a chance to see that everyone behaves differently as well. Some people are talkers, some are quiet, and some are in between those two extremes, but you have to allow people to be who they are.

As a father/coach/teacher I recognized how to talk to

each child/player/student because I had to know the best way that each particular person receives the information I was giving. I believe in the mantra of **say it, demonstrate it, and then let them do it** when it comes to teaching a skill or lesson. Even then someone may not get it but as long as you show patience with them they will give it their best shot to learn it.

Now, I want to give some advice to kids going through what I did who may read this or anyone who may deal with those types of kids. The first piece of advice is when you lose a parent by death, abandonment, incarceration, or whatever the case may be. YOU ARE NOT ALONE.

You may hear it a lot but there are people like me who understand what you'll be going through and would like to help you. Like I mentioned earlier, when I was a young kid there were many times when I felt like I was going through the pain alone. But as I got older and looked back on many instances, there were people helping me deal with it in their own way. They weren't necessarily talking to me about what I was feeling, but they were giving me support by helping me in a lot of other ways.

As I said in the beginning of the book, counseling wasn't a solution that many people in my family or community received. If someone was getting counseling they were considered "crazy" or "something is wrong" with them.

In my dad's hometown of Columbia, North Carolina there were a lot of older people who knew my dad and there were friends of his who made sure I was okay with certain things. My godfather Billy "Wood" Barber used to own a nightclub in Columbia called Club Disco 64 and there would be times when he saw me walking down the street without a haircut. He would grab me (basically snatch) and take me into the barbershop that was near his club. He would tell the barber (Mr. Warren) to cut my hair and then give me the change that was left after the haircut.

He was basically paying me to get a haircut, now that's some funny stuff. He taught me many other things as well, but I just remember how he was always doing things like that for me and I appreciated him so much.

My mom's brothers James, George, and Tim Honablew were like that with me as well because they helped me deal with a lot of things I was going through without saying much. I just hated being around my uncle James when wrestling would come on because he would always grab whichever youngster was close and do a wrestling move on us.

My uncle Tim who passed away last year was the quiet

unassuming one who always had a smile on his face and didn't cause any trouble. He was very knowledgeable about sports and when he said something about a team or player I took heed to it. He was one of the biggest UNC Tar heels fans around and the only Kansas City Chiefs fan that I knew.

    My uncle George who I have looked up to the most is the one who doesn't care about what anyone says and will be himself no matter who is around. He used to tell me stories about how he would visit us when we were living in New York. Which I didn't know about because I was too young to remember that we lived in New York when I was first born. They all were into sports and my love for it started because of them.

    I also had friends who knew that I had lost my father and probably saw me act out on occasions, but were still my friends no matter what. Especially the friends who knew me from pre-school all the way through high school. They just accepted me for who I was and I've always appreciated them for that.

Look at some of the people I mentioned from chapter three, there are millions of people who can relate and are willing to share their stories.

The next piece of advice I will give is ACCEPT THE FACT THAT LIFE IS NOT FAIR. You will have challenges in your life that CAN make you mentally and emotionally stronger, IF you realize that's what those moments are meant for.

Not having one or both of your parents is one of life's huge challenges that will test your resolve. It's a void that can't be filled but you can still achieve the happiness you want out of life. I don't want to minimize the pain you'll feel at times because I have missed my dad every day of my life since he died, but I have grown strength from it.

I could have made myself a victim and just gone through life without any ambition or motivation, saying how unfair it is that he was taken away from me. However, I wouldn't be here telling my story and the story of so many others if I hadn't moved forward with my life.

There were many days I've spent crying just thinking about my father and I still have those days now. I have been living on 44 years of good memories about my dad. I'm sure he had his failings as a man and as a father but I didn't see any of those things. All I felt from my dad was love, a feeling that playing sports also gave me.

I have ALLOWED myself to have those moments of pain thinking about him and then I move on or else I would be in a permanent position of sorrow, which is a depressing place to be.

The final piece of advice I want to give is find something positive that will mentally, physically, and spiritually (regardless of who and what you believe in) HELP you get over that very empty feeling of loss. I touched on this a great deal in Chapter 10, discussing how Sports became therapy for ME and is the whole premise for writing this book.

I know for a fact that there are many athletes (high school, collegiate, and pro) who are dealing with mental health issues that weren't addressed when they were younger. For some of us, sports has been like a fantasy world to get away for a while from the pain we've been dealing with. Sports is a better alternative than things such as drinking alcohol, taking drugs, or any other negative outlet that some

SPORTS HEAVEN

people use to mask the pain they're feeling.

I've never been drunk or high, but I'm sure those things could not make me feel the satisfaction or excitement I got from competing in sports. Hearing crowds go wild or people cheer when you do something well on the court is something I can't explain. The only word I can think of is heavenly. I am the person I want to be because sports helped to mold me into that.

SPORTS HEAVEN

Me with my daughter Bria when she was 3. Daddy's girl for life! A beautiful, smart, and talented grown woman now.

SPORTS HEAVEN

Me and my oldest son Cam when he was a year old. Today he is so smart, handsome, and mature for someone who clowned around so much as a kid.

SPORTS HEAVEN

Me and my son Chance hanging around the Hulk at a museum in New York. He has a lot of potential much like his older brother and sister.

SPORTS HEAVEN

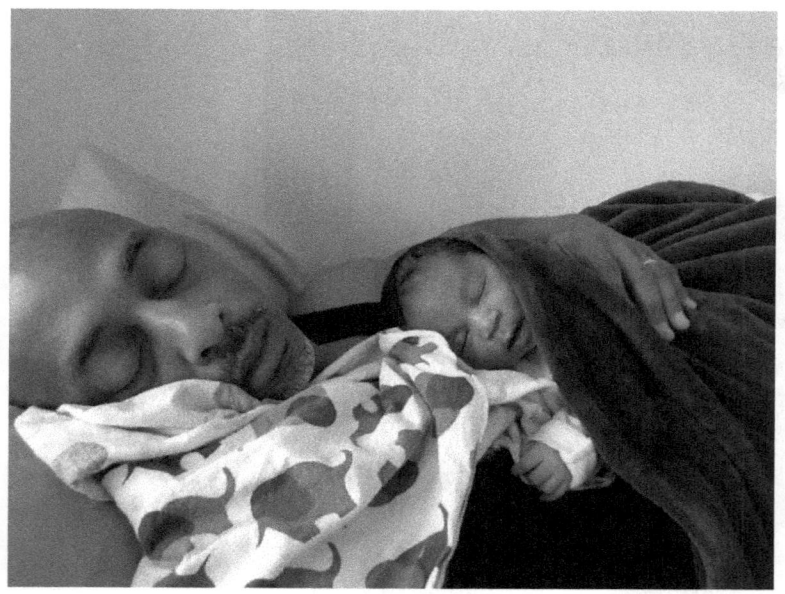

Me sleeping with my son Maverick on my chest. Something I have done with all of my kids even though I was told it would "spoil them."

SPORTS HEAVEN

Chapter 0: Sports Heaven versus Reality

"I found my heaven on earth with sports…."

When I think about the number zero the first thing that comes to my mind is the end of a game. Time counts down in sports not up, and in life you can't get time back. Most coaches will say "play until the clock hits zero" which means you play hard until the game is over. This is also a pretty good way to approach life.

Even with numbers, sports concepts are present in my way of thinking, so it is only right that my book ends with chapter zero. I remember my car tag numbers by thinking about some of my favorite athletes. The last four numbers on one of my car tags was 5692 so I remembered it by thinking about football players Lawrence Taylor (number 56) and

SPORTS HEAVEN

Reggie White (number 92).

All of the things that I have mentioned that sports has provided me from Chapters 10 to 1 are just "the tip of the iceberg" in terms of why sports is a haven for kids missing some parental guidance. There are many other reasons why sports can be a place of refuge.

A child eventually becomes a man or woman IF their life is able to progress with age. For most Fatherless/Motherless children, there are a lot of outside influences that may prevent them from becoming productive adults or adults at all. This is where sports becomes a buffer from some of those influences.

Many fatherless/motherless children have to deal with crime ridden communities, areas where drugs are sold and abused, high unemployment, bad education, limited opportunities in their surroundings, financial distress, food "deserts", and other barriers to healthy living.

The area of Eastern North Carolina where I grew up didn't have much crime, but many of the other barriers I mentioned we had. I can't count the number of times I was offered alcohol or marijuana by someone when I was younger, but someone else would step in and would say "he doesn't do that!" The people stepping in believed that I had a better future than what was presently going on at that time so they protected me.

I didn't have a problem saying "no" myself because I didn't want to be involved with those things. I don't know how they were able to get alcohol, but I remember seeing a lot of high school students drinking when I was in high school, the same with smoking. When I hear people my age or older now say things like "these kids these days….." All I can think is, some of the same things they do today were going on when I were younger.

I prided myself on staying away from drugs and alcohol, but the others that protected me saw that I had potential with basketball that could help my future. Would it have been the same without it? I'm not sure, but I know that played a part in me staying away from bad things and them wanting to help keep it that way. So sports gave me some protectors.

The area where I grew up was and still is one of the poorest areas in North Carolina and I knew many people who worked on farms. As mentioned previously in Chapter 7, I worked on a farm before and it was my first job. I hated it and I told myself many times that I wasn't going to stay in that area to do that kind of work as an adult.

I knew some hard working people who did that kind of work, but the pay was low and there weren't any benefits. I think they only did it because they didn't have more education or there weren't any other opportunities for them.

You can go into almost any inner city and it's the same issues as the rural country areas, lack of opportunities. If every other sector in the world provided the same opportunities and support that sports does, then maybe there would be other havens for kids who were like me. But for many years and currently that's not the case.

I didn't personally know any doctors, lawyers, engineers, or any other white collar professionals when I was growing up, so those occupations weren't ones that I thought about becoming.

SPORTS HEAVEN

The idea of entering one of those professionals didn't occur to me until I got to college and I thought that I could become a lawyer (my first major was actually Sociology/Pre-law). I didn't become a lawyer, but the opportunity and the ability to do so were available to me.

Growing up I remember my grandparents used to grow their own vegetables, and had a pear tree in the front yard. We even had a corn field next to our house and an older relative who used to grow grapes. Vegetables and fruits were almost mandatory in our diets and I thought that was normal for everybody until I went to visit my stepfather in Norfolk, Virginia one summer.

There were hardly any stores that sold vegetables or fruits in the area near his house and there weren't any gardens. That whole summer after playing basketball with friends I met there we would go get candy and other sweets which was very different from what I did back home in Carolina.

Now I ate a lot of candy in Carolina with my friends, but we ate more vegetables and fruits than we did candy. I didn't understand why there was a difference until I got older and I heard some scholars discussing the term "food deserts."

There are a lot of athletes who grow up or have grown up in areas like that. Which is why it is important that they become athletes or at the least exercise, in order to help negate the diets in which they are accustomed.

When I saw or heard the word diet I always thought that someone was trying to lose weight by lowering their calories and eating less food. I didn't know anyone who discussed the importance of a healthy diet and most people I knew ate whatever they wanted. Many people weren't considering the dangers to their health because of the food they were eating.

But in athletics, diet took on a whole new meaning because it was something that was discussed in how athletes took care of their bodies for optimal performance. It has been taken to a higher level with athletes today and I think it is a great thing.

I didn't understand the importance of taking care of my body until I started playing sports and I realized you have to be in shape in order to compete. I also didn't see many people in my community exercising just to stay in shape, so physical fitness wasn't necessarily a focus.

Sports made me consider the importance of exercising and gave me a lifelong love of working out even after my playing days were over.

If I wasn't involved with sports, I don't know what I would have been doing with my "free time" because there wasn't much else I was interested in and there wasn't much else to do in my town. We didn't have recreation centers or any other places for kids to go play, so playing sports in someone's backyard was the best option for me and my friends.

It doesn't take much to find trouble and there are certain types that can derail a person's future in the worst way. The ones I'm thinking about involve criminal activity and there are a million stories of young athletes who had potential to at least compete at the college level, but decided to get involved with the wrong things.

This is another important aspect of why sports is a

refuge because it provides a place for young boys and girls to stay away from the trouble around them. There are many instances where kids aren't trying to get into trouble, but it "finds them" and sometimes it can be fatal. I read some heartbreaking articles this year on some college basketball prospects getting gunned down in their neighborhoods. This has been happening for a long time and I was a teenager when the exact same thing occurred to highly regarded basketball prospect Ben Wilson in Chicago.

When I was a teenager, I know my mom felt better when basketball season was happening. She didn't have to wonder where I was, she knew I was at the gym. It's a feeling many parents can relate, but imagine how a parent must feel when they live in an area where there's drugs and violence. That football field, tennis court, basketball gym, and other athletic playing areas provide a place of safety for some kids from their environments.

Now take into account the mental strain placed on kids that endure these negative things in their environment daily, and how it impacts their mentality. There are some collegiate and professional athletes right now who probably have developed PTSD (Post Traumatic Stress Disorder) because of what they endured during their childhoods.

What is something that can change that way of thinking after seeing so much negativity? What can make them think they can overcome all of these odds?

Of course you know I'm going to say sports because that's what it was for me. But it could be music, art, or education for someone else. Being around negativity all the time is stressful and depressing, so being involved in sports

SPORTS HEAVEN

has many mental benefits for someone looking to "get away" from that.

The reality of my life is that I always felt like the odds were against me and it seemed like those odds increased after the death of my father. Because of sports I learned how to overcome odds because that is one of the important lessons that it teaches you.

After my father's death there were times when I was looking to be "saved" or for a savior until I fully grasped that I just needed the person in the mirror to grow and mature. The cover on this book (it's a boy growing into a man from my eyes) signifies my growth in life and how I found my heaven on earth with sports.

SPORTS HEAVEN

Me with 2 kids from my Total Skills Basketball Camp at my old high school. I want to do all I can for as long as I can to help kids who grew up like me.

SPORTS HEAVEN

Epic Dialogue (Epilogue)

At the beginning of this book you may have or should have noticed that the chapters started at 10 and ended at 0. One of the reasons I did it is because I wanted my book to be different because I enjoy being different.

The main reason I did it is because when my father's life ENDED it marked the BEGINNING of a different journey in life for me, so all of my life I have embraced different. Sometimes things in life doesn't happen in the order we expect and you have to be prepared for that.

This book has been a long time in the making, I started this book in 2015 when I was 45 and now it's 2020(yeah I'm now the Big 5-0!). Getting 50 in a basketball game is something I always wanted to do but I didn't think much

SPORTS HEAVEN

about reaching the age of 50, especially since my father died when he was 39.

Reaching 40 and 50 was a big blessing in my eyes because of all the death I've seen, I didn't know if I would get this far. My son Cameron even told me one time that he was afraid to turn 6 years old because he knew that is when my father died. He was afraid it would happen to us.

The truth is, that is something I used to think about as well but I didn't want to tell my kids that. And to think, I used to think that 40 and 50 were old people until I reached those numbers.

I didn't have any idea of how hard it is to write a book and I thought I would have had it done years ago, but I understand fully that some things aren't as easy as they seem. I commend anyone who does writing for a living because you have to put time into it on a daily basis and that is something I haven't been able to do.

I just knew that I wanted to tell my story and the story of many others no matter how long it took me do it. In 2018 my son Maverick was born so a lot of time has been spent

SPORTS HEAVEN

getting him acclimated into this world. 2020 has gotten off to a rough start to put it mildly and we have experienced things that we haven't seen in our lifetimes with this virus.

First, the death of Kobe Bryant with his daughter Gianna and 7 other passengers (including the pilot) on January 26th was a shock to the sports world and world in general. I've shed many tears over that tragedy like many others. I wasn't a big Kobe Bryant fan, but I was always impressed with the skills and work ethic he possessed. Even though I personally believe that a good work ethic should be a requirement for everybody, not just professional athletes.

When the media was reporting the news of his death my heart was broken for his wife and kids, especially for his kids because the thought of them losing their father hurt me. Once I found out his daughter and some other girls her age had also been involved it hurt even more.

This is what passed through my mind: If there is a Heaven and I lived well enough for entry upon my death. If I meet God and my daughter is meeting God with me, I would cry before God saying "not my baby, not right now!"

I've lived my life with tragedies since I was young, but EVERY TIME I hear a story about someone dying and leaving kids behind it saddens me because I can relate to the kids. Most parents will tell you that they want to live long enough to see their kids grow to adulthood and become independent. The main reason it's so sad when a parent dies before they are able to help with that process.

The George Floyd and Breonna Taylor tragedies has made some high profile athletes do what I've been hoping would happen for years: Use their platform to help expose a lot of injustices and inequalities that are occurring in our society. I hate those tragedies is what it took for SOME athletes to get involved but I'm happy they're starting to speak up. There is a lot more work to be done. Not saying they are saviors but they have a lot of influence and can help in so many ways.

The truth is many people will listen to them before they listen to others in positions of power. What's going on now is highlighting issues that have plagued society and the sports world for a very long time. A lot of people who have been or are now in positions of leadership within society and sports don't care about the people they lead.

In Chapter 4 I mentioned being a firm believer that athletes should start their own leagues or DEMAND to have people who look like them in positions of power. It's the same

SPORTS HEAVEN

in every part of society, in order to get real change where change is needed you probably have to change the people who are leading. And definitely change some laws!

Skeptics will state that athletes should stick to sports and not get involved in other areas such as politics or social stances, but that is pure ignorance because it is all connected.

Every chapter in this book was designed to illustrate how sports has made me a more well-rounded person, which means I have been able to take the lessons from it and apply it to other areas of my life.

I'm also a Desert Shield/ Desert Storm War Veteran who was in the United States Army and my experiences from sports even helped me during my time in the Middle East. I understood the idea of teamwork and it is never more important when your life is on the line in a war zone, where

SPORTS HEAVEN

you have to rely on the skills or knowledge of someone else. I took the knowledge of working "for the better of the team" from sports into my time in the military.

I was in Saudi Arabia when the Desert Storm war started ON my 21st birthday. Another level of bringing your birthday "in with a bang!"

SPORTS HEAVEN

I'm thankful for everything that sports has given me but at this point of the book I have to thank some people who have inspired me at one point or have been a guiding presence in my life. I can't name them all because there are too many. But every person who has helped me, supported me, or loved me in my lifetime knows that I love them back and I have appreciated them because I have told them.

That's an important thing I have learned from my dad's and other loved ones deaths, that the people you love and care about should know it. There are times in life when we may take people we love or certain things for granted, especially things we feel we're supposed to have.

I have tried to remind myself to be thankful for everything I have in my life and not take anyone or anything for granted. I've been knowing for 44 years that your life can change in an instance, so that has made me love the people who love me and tell them while showing it.

I don't have to go on social media and post that I love someone or say that I appreciate their support, I tell them face to face or over a phone call. Technology has changed the way we interact and communicate with people but I still like doing some things the old way. You have information that's for public consumption and information that's private. I like to keep the two separated so there's not any misunderstandings.

I would like to give special thanks to: My mom who LET me believe I could be whatever I wanted in life and ALWAYS gave encouraging words to whatever I said I was going to do. If I had told my mom I was going to the moon she would probably had said "Good luck and be careful." The spirits of my father, grandparents, and other family members who have passed on that supported me or helped to bring me into this world. My sisters (Alfreda, Alicia, and Sharese) and brothers (Jeffrey and Durrell) who have watched my life's journey from day one. All of my aunts, uncles, cousins, nieces, nephews, and friends who have helped me throughout my life. Big salute to my supportive people from Columbia and Creswell, North Carolina. I have to mention Roper and Plymouth because I had some supportive people from there as well. I'm glad I grew up there and I proudly represent my best for the good people from those areas.

A super special thanks to my wife Annette (definitely my "better half" who has made me better) and my kids who have added so much joy to my life. I can't put into words how much I love you all.

SPORTS HEAVEN

I don't know how the next quarter of my life is going to "play",

but I know I want my wife by my side until the clock runs out.

SPORTS HEAVEN

I appreciate everyone who took the time to read this book and I hope it provided some insight to why sports is important to some of US. The main purpose of this book is to inspire kids who are experiencing what I did or something similar and help give them some motivation for their future. I also know there are some young adults who had similar journeys, so I wanted to speak to them as well.

We all are meant to enjoy our lives and find some happiness in it. Parents are an important guide in helping us become the people we want to be, but sometimes things happen when they are not around to do that. In those instances, you have to find some joy and keep moving FORWARD no matter what.

My son Chance asked me in regards to the cover on the book "Dad, isn't the guy looking at heaven and doesn't

SPORTS HEAVEN

that mean he has to die to get there?" So I told him "no, he has found some heaven on earth." If you haven't found your heaven on earth YET I hope that you do. As for me mine awaits, time to go watch some sports.......

44 years ago my father died, sports has helped me grow.

www.ingramcontent.com/pod-product-compliance
Lightning Source LLC
Chambersburg PA
CBHW060726110426
42738CB00056B/1762